Angela Gray's
Cookery School

Festive Recipes

Photographs Huw Jones

Festive Recipes
Angela Gray's Cookery School
Published in Great Britain in 2017 by
Graffeg Limited

Written by Angela Gray copyright © 2017.
Food photography by Huw Jones
copyright © 2017.
Food styling by Angela Gray.
Designed and produced by Graffeg Limited
copyright © 2017

Graffeg Limited, 24 Stradey Park Business
Centre, Mwrwg Road, Llangennech,
Llanelli, Carmarthenshire SA14 8YP Wales
UK Tel 01554 824000 www.graffeg.com

ISBN 9781912050444

1 2 3 4 5 6 7 8 9

Photo credits

Pages 6-147, cover and end papers
© Huw Jones

Pages 148-156 © A L S Photography
www.alsphotography.co.uk

Angela Gray's

Cookery School

Festive Recipes

Photographs Huw Jones

GRAFFEG

Contents

Canapés

Starters

Mains

Desserts

Introduction

Welcome to my Festive Recipe collection. I have to say, this has been such a joyous experience working through a catalogue of food memories. Looking back, my Mum was so brilliant at making everything special at Christmas and I have taken inspiration from her in creating my own celebrations and traditions.

Each and every recipe has been part of Christmas at some time in my life. Travelling and working in countries such as France, Switzerland and Belgium introduced me to new ideas to share with people back home. Many of these influences together with those I grew up with are threaded throughout this book.

Getting ready for Christmas is all part of the fun in building the festive mood and spirit. In order to keep stress at bay and enjoy the preparation more, there is a lot you can do ahead to save time, money and energy. If you are a traditionalist at heart, you can start with a Christmas pudding and cake. My Mum would always make our pudding and two fruitcakes in October. One cake would become the official decorated one, well fed with brandy, whilst the other, she would say, would give her the extra energy needed to get through all the additional preparations! I know what she meant. Around this time she would also make dozens of mince pies and freeze them, plus chutneys, pickles and relishes, utilising the abundance of late autumn ingredients from the vegetable and fruit garden. Christmas was almost done!

But hold on! I have lots more to tempt you with, so let's start at the beginning with some delicious canapés. I think they are the perfect way to welcome guests and to set the tone of what will follow. I used to make thousands of these with my fellow cooks at Annie Fryer Catering in London, for swanky cocktail parties and receptions at formal dinner or wedding celebrations. So rather than reaching for those poor supermarket imitations, why not make a few varieties yourself and pop them in the freezer for later when you can freshly cook them on the day. I always double up on the recipes so I have plenty to see me through those busy gatherings.

In the "Starters" section you will find some lovely ideas for entertaining. For example, I love presenting a whole side of Gin Cured Salmon (page 26). It's visually beautiful, as you can see from Huw's photographs, and such an impressive crowd pleaser. I recently made the recipe using Dyfi Distillery "Pollination Gin", it is the best Gin I have come across and well worth seeking out. Make it ahead and freeze, it keeps very well for up to 6 weeks.

The "Main Course" section offers a wide selection of dishes where flavour and extravagance rule. These recipes stem from the grand houses where I cooked as a private chef. Ingredients such as wild mushrooms, truffles, chestnuts, citrus, fortified fruits, liqueurs, spirits, nuts, herbs and fois gras would be used in many of the meat-based dishes. The recipes for Ballotine of Goose and Rolled Turkey Crown may initially appear to be a little involved, but just take one step at a time and you will get there and I promise, it will all be worth it.

As I mentioned earlier, I have developed my own festive traditions that are routinely exercised in the run up to Christmas. For example, I have adopted a "Once a Year" rule for my much sought after Raised Pork Pies (people do ask for them in the New Year, but I pronounce that the kitchen door is closed on them until next year!) Also, my Seafood Extravaganza with Thrice Cooked Chips is only ever served either on Christmas or New Year's Eve. The Traditional Spiced Beef is probably the most involved recipe because it takes 16 days of TLC before Christmas Day; 2 days for the sugar rub, followed by 14 days fully immersed in spices and turned each night in the fridge as I brew my bedtime cocoa. All this time invested will yield very special results.

In the "Desserts" section you will find some alternative ideas to the British traditional pudding. I have included a lovely Christmas pud,

but I have always made a couple of additional desserts to keep everyone in the family happy. One of our favourites uses the humble pear, each stuffed with a delicious mix of fruit and nuts, then cooked and soaked in a full-bodied wine flavoured with spices. Another favourite hails from France; a Jalousie is a crisp, buttery puff pastry filled with rich homemade mincemeat and frangipane, topped with cooked slices of apple in Calvados, crowned with a tiara, a suitably dressed finale for the feast.

I hope this book gives you inspiration to create something really special for your festive table. Deciding on your menu in advance will help you to plan the shopping and preparation, which is half the work done. I have included some tips in the back of the book on achieving a stress-free Christmas, and I will be cheering you on through the pages to try something new to wow your friends and family.

Canapés

Deep fried Wontons with Mushroom, Chestnut, Porcini and Parmesan with Parsley

Ingredients

24 wonton skins

Sunflower oil for frying

Filling

25g butter

1 small onion, finely chopped

1 fat garlic clove, pasted with ¼ teaspoon sea salt

2 tablespoons of white wine

Sea salt and black pepper to season

250g chestnut mushrooms, finely chopped

1 heaped teaspoon porcini soaked in a little hot water

1 tablespoon Parmesan, grated – extra for finishing

A few scrapes of nutmeg

1 teaspoon of chopped thyme leaves

2 tablespoons of chopped parsley to finish

Makes 24

What you do

1 Heat the butter, add the onions and slowly fry until soft and a little sticky. Stir in the garlic, cook for 30 seconds and add the wine and bubble for a minute. Add the mushrooms and porcini with juice and cook until the mixture is almost dry. Tip onto a plate to cool down. Once cooled, mix in the Parmesan, nutmeg and thyme, taste and season accordingly.

2 The mixture should be full on in flavour as it must shine through the wonton wrap.

3 Lay a few wonton skins out at a time, lightly wet the edges with water, place ½ a teaspoon of the mixture in the middle and fold in half, sealing the edges. Repeat until all the filling is used up.

4 One third fill a deep pan with sunflower oil and heat up. Test with a cube of bread; it should sizzle gently and brown in approximately 2 minutes.

These are so good and, in my experience, very popular! So I always double up on the recipe and make them ahead. You can open freeze them on a baking tray covered with clingfilm. Once they are frozen, you can pop them in a poly freezer bag for easier storage. You can cook them straight from frozen, they just take a couple of minutes longer.

Spiced Chicken and Chorizo Rolls

Ingredients

300g skinned and trimmed chicken thighs

100g chorizo

100g breadcrumbs

2 tablespoons light oil

1 large onion, finely chopped

2 fat garlic cloves, pasted with sea salt

1 small chilli, finely chopped

1 tablespoon curry powder

1 dessertspoon mango chutney

1 tablespoon chopped coriander

1 pack puff pastry or 1 x quantity shortcrust pastry

1 egg, beaten

Makes 24

What you do

1 Set your oven to 200°C/Fan 180°C/Gas 6.

2 Cut up the chicken thighs and place in a food processor. Chop the chorizo and also pop in the processor together with the breadcrumbs. Whiz to combine and break down.

3 Heat a pan, add the oil and cook the onions until soft – I use a little water to help this along. Brown lightly, then stir in the garlic and cook for a minute. Add the chilli and curry powder and cook to form a paste, adding a little water to help. Add the chutney and coriander and set aside to cool. Tip the chicken mixture into a bowl, add the spiced onion mix and combine.

4 Cut the pastry in half and gently roll out to form a large rectangle. Divide the chicken mixture in half and place in a sausage line at one edge. Brush the opposite edge with egg, roll over and seal. Cut into 12 slices and place on an oiled baking sheet.

5 Repeat with the other half of the pastry and mixture. Brush the top of the slices with egg wash and bake in the oven until puffed and golden in colour – around 25 minutes. Eat hot or cold. Store in a sealed container in the fridge for up to 3 days.

As in the previous recipe, freeze ahead on baking sheets, then bag them up until needed. You can cook them from frozen; they will take an extra 5 minutes to cook through. Once the pastry is golden, turn the heat down to 160°C/Fan 140°C/Gas 3 and cook for a further 5 minutes.

Prawn and Sesame Toasts

Ingredients

400g peeled prawns, drained

1 egg white

1 fat garlic clove, chopped

3 teaspoons light soy sauce

1 tablespoon cornflour

Sprinkle of fine sea salt

2 spring onions, chopped

1 finger of ginger, grated

6 slices white bread, crusts trimmed off

2 beaten eggs with a little water

Sesame seeds

Cooking oil as needed, for deep frying

Makes 36 toasts

What you do

1 Put all ingredients except the bread, the sesame seeds and the 2 beaten eggs in a food processor and blend to a paste.

2 Spread the paste on 1 side of the bread and press down as much as possible. Cut into 6 rectangles.

3 Dip the prawn side into egg then press into sesame seeds.

4 Heat 4 inches of oil in a pan or wok (I use a deep frying pan), until hot but not smoking. Place your toasts into the oil and fry for 30 to 50 seconds each side until golden. Drain well on kitchen paper before serving.

When you serve these, they will disappear very quickly, so make lots of them! Freeze ahead as in the previous recipes. Cook straight from frozen, just test one of them when they turn golden to ensure they are hot all the way through.

Sweet Potato Fritters and Spicy Dip

These are so easy to make and can be part cooked until lightly golden, cooled, and then frozen as in the previous recipes. You will literally have a party waiting to happen in your freezer!

Ingredients

150g grated potato

120g onion, thinly sliced

2 large cloves garlic, pasted with a little sea salt

300g sweet potato, coarsely grated

1 teaspoon sea salt

2 medium eggs

4 sprigs mint, leaves chopped

6 sprigs parsley, chopped

¼ teaspoon black pepper

50g self raising flour

Sunflower oil for frying

Makes 24-30
small fritters

What you do

1 Place all the ingredients in a bowl and mix together. You may need a little more flour depending on the moisture level in the vegetables. The finished mixture should be creamy in consistency.

2 Heat a large pan $\frac{1}{3}$ filled with sunflower oil and pop a little of the mixture in to test the heat. When it starts to sizzle, add dessert spoonfuls of the mixture, about 6 at a time, and cook until golden. Turn over to complete the cooking.

3 Drain well on double-layered kitchen paper.

4 Serve with a bowl of shredded winter salad and the spicy dip, or a dollop of strained yoghurt to dip into.

Spicy Dip

Ingredients

200ml good mayonnaise

200ml Greek style yoghurt or soured cream

1 heaped teaspoon of medium-hot curry paste

1 teaspoon grated garlic

1 tablespoon mango chutney

2 tablespoons lime juice

A few twists of black pepper

1 tablespoon fresh chopped mint.

What you do

1 Simply mix everything together, cover and keep in the fridge until needed.

I serve these piled on a plate with a yummy spicy dip or a simple yoghurt with fresh, chopped mint.

Pizzette topped with Perl Las and Cranberry

I love these little Italian inspired canapés. You can make them all year round using different seasonal toppings. In this recipe I have added a little festive twist, using cranberry relish with some delicious blue cheese.

Ingredients

Dough

375g bread flour

5g fast action yeast

5g caster sugar

1 level teaspoon sea salt

60ml olive oil

Approximately 200ml hand hot water

For baking

2 tablespoons polenta

Topping

150g Perl Las (Caws Cenarth) or a nice tasty blue alternative

100g Cranberry relish

24 flat leaf parsley leaves, for garnishing

Makes 24

What you do

1 Put all the ingredients for the pizzette into a food mixer with a dough hook. Mix for 6 minutes on the first speed. The dough should be very soft and quite sticky. Turn the dough out onto a work surface, dimple with your fingers and fold over. Loosely cover with a dry cloth and leave to rest for 20 minutes.

2 Note: If working by hand, mix with a wooden spoon, rotating the bowl as you do so for about 5 minutes, then work it for another 5 minutes with your hands on an oiled surface until the dough is smooth.

3 Lightly flour your work surface and roll out the rested dough thinly. Have ready 2 upturned baking trays and sprinkle liberally with the polenta. Use a 5-6cm diameter biscuit cutter to cut the dough into rounds, then lay them on the baking trays. If you like, you can roll the trimmings of dough into rough

grissini (thin breadsticks) and bake them.

4 Preheat the oven as high as it will go, 220°C/Fan 200°C/Gas 7. Crumble the cheese and divide between the pizzette, keeping it centred, placing a little cranberry relish next to the cheese. Pop the baking tray in the oven and cook in batches for 7-10 minutes. Garnish with flat leaf parsley leaves and serve warm or cold

Cranberry relish

Bring to the boil, then gently simmer 300g of cranberries with 125ml red wine vinegar and 150g sugar for 10 minutes. Add 3 strips of orange or clementine peel, 2 crushed juniper berries and a tablespoon of pomegranate molasses. Pour into a sterile jar and seal. Keep in the fridge until needed.

For a very quick version of this recipe, cut star shapes of medium sliced bread, brush them with melted butter and bake at 200°C/Fan 180°C/ Gas 6 until golden and firm to the touch. Cool and top with the cheese and cranberry relish. Pop back into the oven for 5 minutes, remove, plate and serve.

Gin Cured
Salmon

Ingredients

500g piece of salmon fillet

125g sea salt

25g demerara sugar

Zest of a lemon

2 tablespoons of gin e.g. Dyfi Gin Original, Pollination or Hibernation

3 stems dill

4 stems parsley

Serves 12

I like to offer my guests a shot of the gin straight from the freezer with a little ice and twist of lemon to accompany the salmon.

What you do

1 Mix the ingredients and liberally coat the salmon on both sides. Rub in slightly and place in a plastic food bag, or wrap tightly in cling film.

2 Place the salmon on a flat surface in your refrigerator and weight with whatever is heavy in your fridge – full bottles of juice, litres of milk, etc.

3 Leave in the fridge for 24-48 hours, flipping it over every 12 hours to even the curing process. When ready to eat, remove from plastic wrap, scrape the ingredients off the surface of the salmon, slice thinly, and serve with a delicious salad (see recipe on page 30).

Orange and Pomegranate Salad

This is such a refreshing and colourful salad and a perfect match for a lot of the rich dishes in this book, such as the gammon, especially if it's part of a buffet. I also love it with the Gin Cured Salmon.

Ingredients

4 large oranges

200g kale or green cabbage, trimmed and shredded

1 medium red onion, peeled and thinly sliced and soaked in cold water for 30 minutes

1 large pomegranate – remove the seeds

50g roasted nuts e.g. almonds, hazelnuts or walnuts

A handful of black olives, optional

Dressing

1 clove of garlic, grated

1 tablespoon of sherry or red wine vinegar

1 tablespoon pomegranate molasses

5 tablespoons of fresh orange juice

1 dessertspoon agave or maple syrup

½ teaspoon sea salt

2 tablespoons olive oil

Serves 4-6

What you do

1 Remove the skin from the oranges with a serrated knife and cut into slices, reserving any juice that escapes!

2 Mix together all the ingredients for the dressing and mix half of it with the kale for 30 minutes. This will soften it.

3 After 30 minutes, drain the onions and mix half with the kale. Stir in half of the pomegranate seeds. Spread this mixture over a large serving plate. Arrange the slices of orange on top, finish with the remaining onions, pomegranate seeds, the nuts and olives. Spoon over the remaining dressing and serve.

If you can find blood oranges, use them, or mix with regular oranges, alternating the slices for a really dramatic, colourful effect.

Potted Cheese Pâté with Melba Toasts

This makes a great sharing starter or equally a lovely addition to a buffet table when you have a gathering. I love to serve it with an old favourite, Melba Toast, perfect for scooping up the soft pâté without filling you up too much.

Ingredients

1 x 400g kilner jar

150g cream cheese

100g soft goat's cheese

40g blue cheese

1 fat garlic clove, pasted with sea salt

¼ teaspoon ground black pepper

1 tablespoon white wine

1 tablespoon mixed chopped herbs – sage, rosemary, thyme

Topping

50g sultanas

50ml sherry

150g molasses sugar

2 tablespoons sherry vinegar

2 figs

1 Bay leaf

Serves 8

What you do

1 Mix together the cheeses with the garlic, pepper, wine and herbs and spoon into a sterilised jar. I like to use Kilner style clip top jars.

2 Topping – Heat the sherry, molasses and sherry vinegar together and boil until the liquid becomes a little heavier, syrup like. Add the sultanas, quarter the figs and add them to the molasses. Leave to cool. Spoon over the potted cheese and finish with the bay leaf.

3 This will be good in the fridge for up to a week and tastes great after 48 hours once all the flavours have mingled.

Good Old Fashioned Melba Toasts

Ingredients

6 slices of ready sliced wholemeal or white bread

What you do

1 Preheat your grill to medium heat level. Toast the slices of bread in batches on a baking sheet until golden on both sides.

2 Next, use a serrated knife to remove the crusts, then slice each toast horizontally through its centre, creating two thin sheets of toast.

3 Cut each slice of toast in half diagonally, making them into triangles. Pop them back onto the baking sheet, untoasted-side up, and grill until golden – do this in batches if necessary. Leave toasts to cool.

4 You can store them in an air-tight container for up to 48 hours and re-crisp them in a low oven, 140°C/Fan 120°C/Gas 1, for 5-7 minutes.

Fruit, Nut and Cheese Wreath

I love this recipe, and we make lots of them every year at our festive events. It really looks lovely when it's baked and presented studded with fruity jewels and nuts.

Ingredients

400g bread flour

100g rye flour

10g sea salt

7g easy bake yeast

350-400ml warm water

Filling

1 tablespoon Dijon mustard

½ teaspoon chilli powder

1 tablespoon chopped rosemary leaves

150g toasted nuts, finely chopped e.g. almonds, hazelnuts, walnuts

75g dried fruit e.g. raisins, cherries, cranberries, apricots

75g strong flavoured grated cheeses e.g. Gruyère, mature cheddar, Stilton

To finish

Egg wash

1 teaspoon chopped nuts

1 tablespoon grated cheese

Serves 8-10

What you do

1 Take a large mixing bowl, pop both flours in and mix together by hand.

2 Add the dried yeast and mix through, followed by the sea salt. Make a well in the centre, add ¾ of the water and begin to mix in with your hand. Do not over mix before adding in enough of the remaining water to make a smooth dough.

3 Lightly oil your work surface and throw the dough to extend in front of you, roll it back, pick up and then repeat. Continue the throwing process for about 5 minutes until smooth and tight elastic in consistency. Alternatively, you can mix the dough in a stand mixer using a dough hook and mix for 4 minutes until smooth and elastic.

4 Pop into an oiled bowl or on an oiled tray and cover. Place in

a proving drawer, oven setting at 40°C, or in a warm place. Leave to double in size.

⑤ Preheat the oven to 220°C/Fan 200°C/Gas 7.

⑥ Turn the dough out onto a lightly floured surface and gently knead to get rid of any excess air. Flour your surface and roll out into a large rectangle. Spread the dough with the mustard, sprinkle with the chilli powder, then the rosemary, nuts, dried fruit and finally the grated cheese.

⑦ Roll up like a Swiss roll and have the seam side down on your surface. Cut the roll in half lengthways to produce all the layers. Join the halves together at one end, pressing to seal them, and then pass one over the other all the way to the other ends. Bring both ends together and press in place to form the wreath.

⑧ Lightly flour a baking sheet, place the wreath on and brush with egg wash, sprinkle with the nuts and cheese. Bake for 30-35 minutes until risen and golden. The dough wreath should be golden on the bottom and hollow when you tap it.

⑨ Place onto a cooling rack. Delicious served with soup, a ploughman's lunch or cheese board.

My family are cheese lovers, so I always bake this to serve with a simple cheese board and they love it.

Mini Terrines for Boxing Day

These are packed full of flavour and reminiscent of the terrines I would prepare for the Christmas holidays when I worked in France.

Ingredients

200g chicken or duck livers

300g minced pork shoulder

200g piece streaky bacon, cut into lardons

4 fat garlic cloves, grated

2 medium shallots, finely diced

1 tablespoon thyme leaves

1 small bunch parsley, finely chopped

1 tablespoon pistachios, roughly chopped

50ml brandy or cognac

¼ teaspoon ground cloves

¼ teaspoon ground mace

¼ teaspoon ground ginger

1 ½ teaspoons sea salt

1 level teaspoon ground black pepper

12 slices prosciutto ham

12 port soaked prunes

Makes 6 large or 12 small terrines

What you do

1 Clean the chicken livers – cut away any sinew, blood or green bits, chop into small cubes and place half in a mixing bowl, reserving the rest for layering. Add the minced pork, bacon, garlic, shallot, thyme, parsley, pistachio if using, brandy and the spices.

2 Season and mix well with your hands. If you have time, you can cover and set aside in the fridge for the flavours to mingle for a few hours or overnight.

3 Line the base and sides of 6 large muffin tins or 12 cupcake tins with a disc of parchment, butter and a length of parchment to lift out the terrine when cooked. Then, carefully line the base and sides of the tin with the prosciutto, leaving some hanging over the side and

a few slices for the top. Pack half the meat mixture down into the terrine and press down. Lay a row of chicken livers and insert a prune in the middle and then top with the rest of the meat mixture and press down. Lay the remaining prosciutto over the top and cover with buttered foil.

4 Heat oven to 170°C/Fan 150°C/Gas 5.

5 Lay some folded newspaper sheets to form a thick mat for the tray to sit on top of it in a deep roasting tin. Boil a kettle and pour in enough water so it comes halfway up the muffin/cupcake tin. Carefully place it on the middle shelf of the oven and cook for 30-35 minutes. The internal temperature should be 70°C (using a meat thermometer).

6 Remove the tin from the oven, take the terrines out of the roasting tin and leave to cool completely. Serve with toasted bread – a favourite of mine is walnut bread and some nice winter leaves dressed with walnut oil. You can keep the terrines wrapped up for up to two days.

The smaller terrines are a good starter size, the larger ones can be sliced and served for a buffet. If you wish you can make a large centrepiece terrine by using a 900g terrine tin and making 1 ½ times the recipe. Cook for 1 hour, check the core temperature with a meat probe and remove when it reaches 70°C.

Pickled Pears

I make these every year; they are a little different to the usual pickles or fruit chutneys and look so elegant when decanted into a nice glass dish. They are always on my buffet table accompanying cold meats or cheese. I also use ½ a pear as part of a starter such as the Boxing Day Terrines or the Cheese Pâté.

Ingredients

750g of small "Rocha" pears

450g granulated sugar

400ml cider vinegar

2 sprigs rosemary

2 strips of lemon zest

2 strips of orange zest

4 cloves

4 allspice berries

1 stick of cinnamon

Serves 6-8

What you do

1 Peel the pears and break the cinnamon stick in half.

2 Take a large heavy based pan and add all of the ingredients except the rosemary and pears. Bring slowly to the boil.

3 Add the pears and simmer for 10 minutes. Add the rosemary sprigs and cook for a further 5 minutes.

4 Using a slotted spoon transfer the pears, rosemary and spices to a sterilised jar.

5 Return the liquid to the heat and boil for 5 minutes.

6 Remove from the heat and pour over the pears, rosemary and spices.

7 Seal the jar and store for up to 2 months in a cool dark place. Once opened, keep chilled and eat within 2 weeks.

(8) Label with instructions and serving suggestions e.g. excellent with a nice cheese board, cold cuts and the mini terrines.

Why not consider making these as gifts. They are easy to prepare and cook and look so lovely nestling in a clip top jar. You can wrap them in cellophane and label them with a little serving suggestion.

Smoked Salmon and Lobster Roll with Salad

This is a little bit of luxury and makes a stunningly simple starter for a special supper party. I serve it with a lovely seasonal salad and some good old fashioned Melba Toast.

Ingredients

400g sliced smoked salmon

200g cooked spinach leaves

Sprinkle of sea salt

400g hot smoked salmon, flaked

200g full fat cream cheese

2 tablespoons crème fraîche or 4 tablespoons double cream

2 tablespoons lemon juice

Zest of ½ a lemon

¼ teaspoon black pepper

1 tablespoon chopped herbs such as dill, chives and parsley

1 teaspoon Dijon mustard

¼ teaspoon cayenne pepper

2 cooked lobster tails, meat only, cut lengthways

Serves 8

What you do

1 Place two sheets of cling film on top of each other and line with the smoked salmon overlapping slightly.

2 Cover with the spinach leaves and sprinkle with a little sea salt and black pepper.

3 Pop the following ingredients into a mixing bowl – hot smoked salmon, cream cheese, crème fraîche, lemon juice, zest, pepper, herbs, mustard and cayenne pepper. Mix really well and spread over the spinach, but leave a little border all around.

4 Place the 4 sections of lobster tail down the middle.

5 Roll up starting at one edge and roll over tightly. Tuck in the edges and continue until you have a tight cylinder. Twist the cling film at the edges and place in the fridge until you are going to serve it. It will need at least an hour, but overnight is best.

6 Remove the clingfilm, slice into 8 equal portions and serve on starter plates. Serve with a lovely winter leaf salad.

Lovely Salad

Ingredients

8 handfuls of mixed leaves, choose from pink or white chicory, endive, radicchio and watercress

8 stems of flat-leaf parsley leaves, torn

2 giant gherkins, finely chopped

Dressing

2 heaped teaspoons Dijon mustard

2 teaspoons maple syrup

½ teaspoon sea salt

2 garlic cloves, grated

2 tablespoons red wine vinegar – Cabernet red is delicious

12 tablespoons olive oil

4 tablespoons chilled water

Serves 8

What you do

1 To make the dressing, put all the ingredients in a jar with a tight-fitting lid and shake until smooth, creamy and yellowish-green in colour. Adjust the salt or vinegar to your taste: if you find it a little too sharp, add another teaspoon of maple syrup. Leave for about 20 minutes so that the ingredients mingle nicely.

2 Wash and drain the salad leaves and pat off excess water with kitchen paper, then place in a salad or mixing bowl. Mix in the parsley leaves and serve with the dressing.

3 If you don't use all the salad, pop it in a poly bag and keep in the fridge, it will stay crisp for a couple of days. You can also keep the left over dressing in a screw top jar in the fridge for a good week.

Raised Pork Pie

Ingredients

Pastry

500g plain flour

160ml water

120g butter

70g lard

1 level teaspoon salt

Filling

25g butter

1 medium onion, chopped finely

½ an eating apple, diced

2 sticks of celery, trimmed and chopped

100ml ginger wine

1 tablespoon mixed herbs – sage, parsley

1 teaspoon Dijon mustard

½ teaspoon ground mace

50g breadcrumbs

100g mature cheddar cheese, diced

450g minced pork

200g minced veal or sausage meat

100g cooked ham, shredded

Serves 8

What you do

First make the filling

❶ Melt the butter, add the onion and cook until soft – add a little water to speed up the cooking process. When soft, cook off the water and lightly brown.

❷ Add the apple/celery and cook for 5 minutes, pour in the ginger wine, add the herbs, mustard and mace, cook for 2 minutes then tip into a bowl to cool.

❸ Add the breadcrumbs, cheese and meats and mix through.

Pastry

❶ Place the flour into a large bowl and set aside.

❷ Pour the water into a small pan,

place over a medium heat, add the butter, lard and salt, stirring as the fat melts. Once it comes to the boil, take the pan off the heat and pour it into the centre of the flour.

❸ Stir the mixture with a wooden spoon until all the ingredients are combined. You should now bring the dough together with your hands - be careful as it will be hot! Push together into a smooth dough. Place on a floured work surface and roll out to the thickness of a £1 coin.

❹ Grease an 8" springform cake tin and line the base with baking parchment, or make individual pies in muffin moulds. Line the tin/moulds with the two-thirds of the pastry, reserve the rest for the lid/s.

❺ Fill the tin with the meat mixture and pack in. Roll out the remaining pastry to create the lid. Brush the edge of the pastry in the tin with egg wash and ease the pastry lid in place.

❻ Press the edges together just inside the tin to create a classic domed pie effect. Trim the excess pastry, leaving enough to crimp an impressive stand-up collar. Make a small cross in the centre of the pie and insert the end of a wooden spoon handle to make a shallow hole. Brush with egg wash and bake at 180°C/Fan 160°C/Gas 4 for approximately 1 hour – the juices should run clear from the hole in the top of the pie. Remove and cool. Keep refrigerated and eat within 4 days.

❼ Serve it with some simple pickled vegetables, mustard and chutney.

My top tip here is to make 2 pies, at least! They really are so delicious, and once you cut into one, it will be gone, gone, gone!

Festive Risotto Terrine with Mushroom and Red Wine Jus

A good flavoured risotto is so comforting and I have turned my favourite recipe into layers of deliciousness. It looks so good when it is sliced, revealing all the colours and textures within.

Ingredients

Risotto Base

25g butter

1 tablespoon olive oil

1 medium onion, finely chopped

1 fat garlic clove, finely chopped

150g chestnut mushrooms, thinly sliced

2 tablespoons white wine

200g Arborio rice

20g dried, chopped porcini mushrooms

500ml hot good vegetable stock such as Swiss Marigold

75g grated Parmesan

A handful of chopped herbs – sage, rosemary, thyme

Layering

50g butter

3 large field mushrooms, thickly sliced

12 long thick strips of butternut squash (to fit the terrine tin)

200g wilted spinach

Sea salt, black pepper and grated nutmeg to season

300g Mozzarella, taleggio or blue cheese

75g breadcrumbs, 1 dessertspoon herbs and 1 tablespoon Parmesan cheese for lining the tin and topping the terrine

Serves 6

....

What you do

1 Make the risotto – Heat the butter and olive oil, add the finely chopped onion, cook until transparent, but not coloured. Stir in the garlic and mushrooms and cook until soft. Add the wine and stir in the rice, coating well with the pan juices. Stir in the porcini and start to add the stock a little at a time, about a ladle-full and stir through until absorbed. Repeat this process until all of the stock is used up and the rice is thick and creamy.

Stir in the Parmesan and herbs and set aside.

2 Heat a large frying pan, add the butter and fry the field mushroom slices until lightly golden on both sides. Remove and set aside. Repeat this with the strips of squash, making sure the strips are soft through. Remove from the heat and season both the mushrooms and squash with a good sprinkle of sea salt, black pepper and nutmeg.

3 To assemble the terrine – Butter a 900g loaf tin and line with a piece of parchment paper that covers the bottom and the sides at each end – this will help remove the terrine with ease.

4 Mix together the breadcrumbs, herbs and cheese. Sprinkle half into the base of the tin and turn the tin around so the crumbs stick to the sides. The rest will form a layer in the base.

5 Arrange 6 slices of mushrooms along the centre, then spoon half of the risotto mixture on top and smooth into place using the back of a spoon. Create a layer of spinach on top, then a layer of squash, finishing with the remaining mushrooms.

6 Top with the remaining risotto, smooth over and top with the remaining breadcrumb mixture. Bake in a preheated oven 180°C/Fan 160°C/Gas 5 for 50 minutes until golden and slightly shrunken away from the tin. Stand for 10 minutes before turning out and slicing.

If you are making this for vegetarians, choose cheeses that are made with vegetarian rennet.

Mushroom and Red Wine Jus

Ingredients

50g unsalted butter

2 shallots, diced super fine

350g assorted mushrooms, such as cremini, oyster, shiitake, chanterelle, or white, trimmed and chopped finely

Leaves from 2 fresh thyme sprigs

Sea salt and freshly ground black pepper

120ml Cabernet Sauvignon red wine

60ml strong porcini liquid, or mushroom stock cube, or both mixed

150ml double cream

1 tablespoon chopped fresh thyme or sage leaves

Serves 6

What you do

1 Heat a large, heavy-based pan, add the butter and, when foaming, add the shallots and cook until a light straw colour. Add the mushrooms and thyme; season with salt and pepper. Stir everything together and cook until browned slightly.

2 Add the red wine, stirring to scrape up any stuck bits; then cook and stir to evaporate the alcohol. When the wine is almost all gone, add the stock. Let the liquid cook down and then take it off the heat. Stir in the cream and herbs and season with salt and pepper.

This is perfect for accompanying the risotto terrine, but also for serving with left over festive meats.

For a delicious and quick vegetarian dish using this jus: roast 6 large field mushrooms, dotted with butter and seasoned. Top each with a teaspoon of herby breadcrumbs and cook until golden, for about 25 minutes at 200°C/Fan 180°C/Gas 6. Serve with the jus.

Fish Fillet in Pastry with Spiced Rice and Lentil Pilaf Wrap

This is such an impressive dish and almost a meal all in one. The aromatic spices and creamy pilaf are a delicious surprise inside the buttery pastry. We have served it many times at the School and people just love it.

Ingredients

The Pilaf

1 tablespoon olive oil

25g butter

2 medium onions, thinly sliced

¼ teaspoon ground cinnamon

½ teaspoon cumin

¼ teaspoon sweet paprika

¼ teaspoon ground allspice

Zest of an unwaxed lemon

1 tablespoon lemon juice

2 fat garlic cloves, grated

1 small bunch parsley, finely chopped, plus extra to garnish

1 small bunch coriander

1 tablespoon toasted flaked almonds (optional)

100g Greek yoghurt

500g fresh cooked rice and puy lentils – use mixed grains, but cook according to packet instructions, drain and cool completely under running cold water, drain well and keep covered in the fridge until needed.

Filling

500g cooked spinach leaves, drained and patted dry

1 block puff pastry

2 tablespoons of breadcrumbs

800g skinless fish fillet e.g. salmon, hake, monkfish

1 small egg, beaten for glazing

1 dessertspoon sesame seeds to finish

Serves 8

....

What you do

1 Heat the olive oil and add the butter, stir in the sliced onions, add 2 tablespoons of water, cover with a lid and cook over a medium heat, stirring occasionally until soft. Remove the lid and continue cooking the onions until lightly golden. Stir in the cinnamon, cumin, paprika, allspice, unwaxed lemon zest, lemon juice, garlic and chopped parsley, cook for a minute.

Now stir in the coriander, almonds and yoghurt. Remove from the heat and stir into the cooked rice – taste and season to your liking. Cover and leave to cool.

2 To assemble, roll out the puff pastry into a large, thin rectangle. Sprinkle the 2 tablespoons of breadcrumbs over the top, spoon half the rice mixture on top and spread out evenly, making sure it is a little larger than the fish fillet. Place the fish fillet along the centre of the rice and season well. Top with the blanched spinach leaves, season and then top with the remaining pilaf. Wet the edges of the pastry with some beaten egg, fold over so the edges meet and seal by pressing all around. Trim away the excess pastry and turn over on to a parchment lined baking sheet so that the pastry seal is on the bottom. Crimp the edges with your finger and thumb, brush with beaten egg and sprinkle with the sesame seeds. Bake in a preheated oven 190°C/Fan 170°C/Gas 5, until

well-risen and golden – about 30-40 minutes. Rest for 10 minutes before slicing. Garnish with the rest of the chopped parsley.

3 Serve with simple seasonal greens such as chard, long stem broccoli or shredded cabbage. I also love steamed carrots or roasted squash, plus a delicious spiced mousseline sauce (see page 70).

Take your time to work through making all the elements of this dish and then bring them all together to create something you will be very pleased with.

Spiced Mousseline Sauce

Ingredients

Spiced butter
175g hot melted butter

¼ teaspoon ground cumin

¼ teaspoon sweet paprika

The sauce
3 tablespoons lemon juice

¼ teaspoon white pepper

3 large egg yolks

To Finish
4 tablespoons light chicken or vegetable stock – cube stock is fine

2 tablespoons double cream

1 large egg white, whisked to soft peaks

8 stems and leaves of coriander, chopped

Serves 6

What you do

1 Heat the butter in a small pan with the cumin and paprika. Allow the butter to boil for 1 minute before using in the sauce.

2 To make the sauce – Whisk the lemon juice, pepper and egg yolks together in a heatproof bowl and then place over a pan of gently simmering water. Warm the yolks for about a minute, stirring all the time, then slowly pour in the hot melted butter in a steady stream until the eggs are thickened. Remove the bowl from the heat and stir in the hot stock and cream, then fold in the egg white to give a light creamy sauce. Finish with the chopped coriander and serve.

Note: You can make the sauce in advance, but stop before you add the egg white in the method. Cool the sauce, cover and chill. When you are ready to serve it, reheat gently over gentle simmering water, then whisk and add the egg white etc.

This sauce is based on a classic Hollandaise and is so luxurious. In addition to serving it with the fish fillet in pastry, I also like it with simple poached fish, such as monk or hake.

Ballotine of Goose

Ingredients

1 free-range goose, de-boned

Sea salt and black pepper for seasoning

Stuffing

50g butter

1 large onion, finely diced

2 sticks celery, finely diced

1 heaped teaspoon orange zest

4 tablespoons orange juice

1 tablespoon brandy

1 small bunch of fresh sage, finely chopped

1 small bunch of parsley, finely chopped

6 ready to eat dried apricots, chopped

1 tablespoon dried cranberries

½ teaspoon allspice

150g breadcrumbs

300g minced pork

100g minced veal (optional) or cooked ham

150g chicken livers – goose if you can

1 medium egg, beaten

2 teaspoons of sea salt and 1 flat teaspoon pepper

12 sage leaves

10 pitted prunes soaked in 100ml port for 48 hours

6 slices cured ham

Sauce

750ml stock, including the juices from the goose and good chicken stock for the rest

1 tablespoon pomegranate molasses

1 teaspoon maple syrup

2 ½ tablespoons arrowroot

4 tablespoons red wine – something you are drinking with the goose

Serves 8-10

What you do

To make the stuffing

1 Heat the butter in a large pan, add the onion and celery, plus 4 tablespoons of water, cover with a lid and sauté over a medium heat, stirring occasionally until softened. Remove the lid and continue cooking until lightly golden in colour.

2 Stir in the orange zest, orange juice, sage and parsley, cook off most of the moisture, then add the brandy and flame or ignite using a long nosed lighter. Once the flames subside, add the chopped apricots and cranberries and stir in the allspice. Remove from the heat and transfer into a large mixing bowl. Leave to cool for 10 minutes.

3 Add the breadcrumbs, minced pork and veal and combine everything together. Chop the livers if using and mix in together with the beaten egg, season with the sea salt and pepper. I like to fry a teaspoon of the stuffing to make sure the seasoning is correct.

To assemble

1 You will need a large piece of foil, 1½ times the size of the goose. You may need two sheets overlapping.

2 Lay a large sheet or 2 of parchment paper on top of the foil and sprinkle with sea salt and black pepper. Scatter a few sage leaves along the centre section of the paper. Lay the boned goose out flat on a board, skin side down, and open out completely, seasoning well with salt and pepper. Lay the slices of cured ham across the breast section. Place half the stuffing on top and make a shallow trench using the side of your hand. Insert the prunes and then top with the remaining stuffing.

3 Using cupped hands along the edges of the stuffing, shape it into a cylinder. Take hold of the parchment paper nearest you, pull towards you and upwards, roll up moving over and forward, tucking in the ends; the seal should be underneath. Bring the rolled goose in parchment towards the edge of the foil nearest you and repeat the process, then twist the ends of the foil tightly to form a firm sealed cylinder.

To cook

1 Place in a preheated oven at 150°C/Fan 130°C/Gas 3 for 20 minutes per 450g. Remove the foil and parchment, cutting with scissors. Drain off the juices and reserve them for the sauce.

2 Place back in the oven and turn up the heat to 200°C/Fan 180°C/Gas 6 and cook until golden brown, basting a couple of times throughout to help the colour. This should take about 25 minutes – factor this time into the total cooking time.

3 Remove from the oven and loosely cover with foil and a couple

of tea towels. Leave to rest for about 30 minutes before carving.

4 Meanwhile, have a stiff drink and make the sauce. Spoon off any fat from the juices (you can keep the fat in the fridge for your next roasties) and pour into a saucepan. You need 750ml of liquid, so top up using chicken stock and any resting juices from the meat. Add 1 tablespoon pomegranate molasses and 1 teaspoon of maple syrup to the stock. Bring to the boil, then reduce to a simmer. Thicken with 2½ tablespoons of arrowroot dissolved in 4 tablespoons red wine. Slowly pour into the simmering stock, whisking as you go until the liquid thickens slightly.

Baked Apples with Red Cabbage

My lovely mum, Betty, introduced our family to these scrumptious baked apples when we first ate goose for Christmas. She always loved to experiment and try something new and this was one of her many triumphs. I have adopted this tradition and always serve them with my ballotine of goose or duck.

Ingredients

Cabbage

800g red cabbage

50g butter

1 star anise

2 cloves

1 stick of cinnamon

50g dark molasses sugar

75ml water

75ml cider vinegar

Sea salt and pepper

Apples

4 nice sized eating apples e.g.
Pink Lady, Orange Pippin

40g butter

2 tablespoons lemon juice

Serves 8

What you do

1 Prepare the red cabbage, remove the ribs from the leaves and shred finely.

2 Melt the butter in a large pan, add the star anise, cloves and cinnamon and cook for 2 minutes. Add the sugar and cabbage and stir well. Pour in the water, vinegar and seasoning, stir well. Cover with a lid and cook slowly for about 2 hours. You may need to add a little water at times to prevent sticking. Stir occasionally.

3 Meanwhile, prepare and roast the apples. Cut them in half around the middle and use the tip of a teaspoon to remove the core and pips. Brush with lemon juice and a slice of the butter. Place in a roasting tin lined with parchment. Roast in the oven at 160°C/Fan 140°C/Gas 4 for 30 minutes.

4 Remove the apples, pile the red cabbage in the middle of them and bake for a further 10 minutes.

Remove and serve with the main attraction.

5 You can assemble the apples with the cabbage, cover and keep in the fridge for up to 48 hours. Re-heat at the same temperature, but cover them with buttered foil. Cook for 20 minutes covered and 10 minutes uncovered.

I sometimes like to add a tablespoon of pomegranate molasses to the cabbage and garnish the apples with a few fresh pomegranate seeds. It really is a lovely touch.

Luxury Individual Beef en Croute with Mushroom and Truffle Sauce

Ingredients

50g butter

4 fillet steaks, each weighing about 300g

1 pack filo pastry

4 tablespoons dried breadcrumbs

Sea salt and black pepper

Beaten egg

Filling

50g butter

1 medium onion, finely chopped

1 clove garlic, grated

1 tablespoon brandy

300g chestnut mushrooms, finely chopped

1 tablespoon porcini mushrooms, chopped

Sea salt and pepper

1 tablespoon truffle paste or oil

1 tablespoon mixed chopped herbs e.g. thyme, tarragon

8 slices Parma ham

Makes 8

What you do

First make the filling

1 Melt the butter, add the onions and cook slowly until soft. Stir in the garlic and cook for 30 seconds. Add the brandy and cook for another 30 seconds. Stir in the mushrooms and cook until soft and all the visible liquid has evaporated. Stir in the porcini and season with salt and pepper. Remove from the heat and stir in the truffle paste and herbs. Cool completely.

To prepare the steaks

1 Cut the fillets in half. Melt half the butter in a large frying pan and seal the beef pieces all over, just lightly colouring them – do 4 at a time, just 1 minute on each side, remove and leave to cool.

2 To assemble, melt the remaining butter – you may need a little extra here. You are going to make 8 money bag parcels, so cut the filo large enough to wrap up the pieces of fillet and the topping. Butter the squares of filo, laying one on top of the other to create pointed edges. Spoon ½ a tablespoon of breadcrumbs in the middle, wrap the fillet in a slice of Parma ham and place on top. Next, spoon an eighth of the mushroom filling on top and pack down nicely. Brush the edges of the filo with beaten egg, draw up to the centre and scrunch together to form the moneybag. Place on a baking sheet lined with parchment.

3 Repeat until all the fillets are used up. I would put 4 parcels on 2 lined baking sheets so that they crisp up and brown nicely. Brush with beaten egg and bake 220°C/ Fan 200°C/Gas 7 for 15 minutes until crisp and golden. Remove and leave to stand for 5 minutes before serving.

Mushroom and Truffle Sauce

25g butter
1 medium shallot, finely chopped
1 tablespoon brandy
100g chestnut mushrooms, finely chopped
1 tablespoon porcini mushrooms, chopped
1 teaspoon truffle paste
1 x 400ml can beef consommé
2 tablespoons double cream (optional)
Sea salt and black pepper to taste
2 tablespoons arrowroot dissolved in 4 tablespoons red wine

What you do

1 Melt the butter in a small pan, add the shallot, stir through and sauté until soft. Add the brandy and flame, using a long-nosed lighter. When the flames die out, stir in the mushrooms, porcini and truffle paste and cook for 2 minutes to evaporate any of the liquid and concentrate the flavour. Pour in the consommé and double cream and bring to the boil. Season to taste with sea salt and black pepper. Thicken with the arrowroot, stirring constantly.

BBQ Stuffed Turkey Crown with a Maple, Quince and Mustard Glaze

I love barbecuing, even at Christmas. It somehow diffuses the stress that can sometimes build in the kitchen. A solitary moment out in the garden with the turkey on the BBQ whilst sipping bubbly is my festive karma!

Ingredients

4kg de-boned turkey crown

Brine

Approximately 6 litres of water

250g Halen Môn sea salt

250g light muscovado sugar

3 tablespoons of mixed coloured peppercorns

1 large cinnamon stick, broken in 2

4 cloves

2 star anise

2 fat cloves garlic, smashed

50g piece of ginger, bashed

2 clementines, quartered

2 bay leaves

2 large onions, quartered

12 stems thyme

For cooking the Turkey

400g pancetta slices for wrapping

1 bunch sage

1 tablespoon garlic paste

50g soft butter

2 medium eating apples, grated

2 tablespoons Dijon mustard

1 tablespoon quince paste or jelly

2 big handfuls of cherry or apple woodchips

Glaze

4 tablespoons cider vinegar

1 tablespoon Dijon mustard

2 tablespoons maple syrup

1 tablespoon quince paste or jelly

1 teaspoon sea salt

½ teaspoon ground black pepper

Serves 8-10

What you do

Brine

1 Pour the water into a large container – I have a big stainless steel bowl for this job. Stir in everything else, followed by the turkey crown. Cover and keep in a very cold place or the fridge for up to 48 hours.

Stuffing and rolling the crown.

1 Remove the turkey from the brine and drain well. Pat dry all over using kitchen paper or a new J-cloth. Take a large piece of foil and place on the work surface. Scatter with sea salt and pepper, followed by a few of the sage leaves. Create a large rectangle of overlapping pancetta, this will form a wrap around the outside of the turkey when it is rolled up.

2 Lay the de-boned turkey crown on top of the pancetta and open out, season the meat with a good sprinkle of sea salt and pepper. Prepare the flavourings for the inside of the turkey; finely chop the remaining sage and pop into a bowl, add the garlic, butter, apple, mustard and quince paste, mix well, spread over the meat.

3 Now roll up the turkey – Pick up the foil at the edge nearest you and roll up the turkey, keeping it tight as you roll forward and over;

you should end up with the join underneath. Discard the foil. Secure with string, tying at evenly spaced intervals: 5-7 ties should do it. Tuck the ends in, run a large piece of string along the length and tie on top at the centre of the turkey to secure the ends. Place in a metal roasting tray.

Smoke and cook on the BBQ

1 Soak 2 good handfuls of wood chips for 30 minutes, ready for smoking. Set your BBQ up and light a full chimney of charcoal briquettes. When the coals are ready, tip them into charcoal baskets and place one at either side of the BBQ kettle, or tip into 2 heaps, one at each side to create an indirect heat. Place the lid on the BBQ and allow the temperature to come to 200°C.

Place a roasting tin or foil tray between the coals to collect the turkey juices and add 200ml water; you can use these to make a simple sauce later. Place the turkey crown in the middle of the grill and quickly add the wood chips directly onto the charcoal, pop the lid on and let the smoking commence. After 25 minutes, reduce the heat to 150°C by adjusting the vents slightly under the BBQ and in the lid. Roast for 2.5 hours, or until the interior temperature of the turkey reaches 75°C.

Make the glaze

1 Simply mix all the ingredients together in a saucepan. Bring to the boil and turn off the heat. Baste the turkey with the glaze at 15-minute intervals during the last hour. This will allow a lovely sticky glaze to build up on the skin.

Once cooked, remove from the BBQ, loosely cover with foil and a couple of teatowels. Rest for 20-30 minutes before carving (the temperature at the core will go up slightly during resting time).

To make a quick sauce

Tip the juices from roasting and resting the meat into a saucepan, add a heaped teaspoon of Dijon mustard and 200ml of white wine, top up to 600ml with some chicken stock, bring to the boil and thicken with 2 tablespoons of arrowroot dissolved in a little white wine or stock.

Cooking this in a conventional oven

You can brine before roasting, but you can't smoke the turkey.

What you do

Set your oven at 150°C/Fan 130°C/ Gas 2. Prepare the turkey as per the recipe. Lay a sheet of baking parchment over the foil and spread with 100g butter before applying the seasoning and sage. Roll up the turkey as stated in the recipe, but leave the foil around it, twist the ends to form a tight cylinder (see the recipe method for the goose on page 72, it's exactly the same). Cook for 20 minutes per 400g, remove the foil and paper for the last 20-30 minutes, pour the juices and reserve for the sauce as before. Increase the temperature to 200°C/Fan 180°C/Gas 6, brush the turkey all over with the glaze. Baste a couple of times as the turkey browns. Remove and rest as above and meanwhile make the sauce.

Follow this one step at a time and you will produce a very special main course. I like to leave my turkey in the fridge for 24 hours once stufed and rolled so that all the flavours mingle nicely. You can also make the glaze ahead of time.

Traditional Spiced Beef with Watercress and Horseradish Sauce

Ingredients

3.5kg rolled brisket beef, boned and trimmed

100g light muscovado sugar

175g Halen Môn smoked sea salt or equivalent

40g ground allspice

1 heaped teaspoon whole cloves

2 tablespoons whole black peppercorns

2 tablespoons juniper berries

4 blades mace

2 bay leaves

2 dried Kashmiri chillies

1 teaspoon cardamom seeds

To cook

300ml hot water

Serves 8-10

What you do

1 Place the brisket on your preparation board and pat dry all over with kitchen paper. Spoon the muscovado sugar on top of the brisket and then rub all over the joint. Place the brisket in a large bowl and cover with cling film. Refrigerate for 48 hours.

2 Mix the smoked sea salt, all the spices, bay leaves and chillies together in a blender or pestle and mortar. Remove the beef from the fridge, pour away any liquid collected in the bowl and gently pat off any excess surface blood. Wash and dry the bowl.

3 Rub the spice mixture into the meat all over, including the ends. Put the brisket back into the bowl, cover with a clean tea towel and cling film and return to the fridge for 12 days. Turn the beef every two days, making sure it is still completely covered in the mixture.

4 To cook the spiced beef, preheat the oven to 140°C/Fan 120°C/Gas 1. Remove the brisket from the bowl and wipe off all the spice mixture and pat dry. Line a large casserole or roasting dish with 2 sheets of thick foil. Put the beef in the dish and pour in the hot water. Cover with several layers of kitchen foil and tuck the edges tightly to seal the meat in, cover with a lid if you have one that fits. Bake for 6 hours.

5 Remove the brisket from the casserole dish and place on a large sheet of greaseproof paper, wrap it up and leave to cool for a couple of hours. Serve with chutney, pickles and crisp baked potatoes. Also, try this watercress and horseradish sauce, it's delicious with the beef.

Watercress and Horseradish Sauce

2 large handfuls of watercress, rinsed and drained

2 tablespoons creamed horseradish

2 large garlic cloves, grated

2 tablespoons sunflower oil

1 tablespoon double cream

½ teaspoon sea salt

½ teaspoon black pepper

125g strained Greek style yoghurt

What you do

1 Put all the ingredients except the yoghurt in a blender or food processor and pulse until smooth.

2 Transfer to a bowl, stir in the yoghurt and mix well. Taste to check the seasoning.

Festive Toad

Ingredients

1 large onion, peeled and thinly sliced

2 tablespoons vegetable oil or a little duck or goose fat if you have any

4 good quality butcher's sausages, cut up (if you have sausage meat stuffing left, use it, but add it in with the turkey)

350g stripped turkey meat

175g stuffing, cut into bite sized pieces

2 sprigs of sage leaves, chopped

100g chestnuts, cut in half

100g cranberries

Batter

350g plain flour

6 medium eggs

375ml milk

Salt and pepper

Serves 6 people – for a crowd I would bake 2.

What you do

1 Set your oven to 200°C/Fan 180°C/Gas 6.

2 Place the sliced onions into the bottom of a baking dish or a small roasting tin, pour in the vegetable oil and mix well. If you are using raw sausages add them to the pan, cover with foil and cook for 15 minutes.

3 In the meantime, make the batter – place the flour in a large mixing bowl, make a well in the centre, break in the eggs and start mixing. Start to pour in the milk slowly and gradually incorporate the flour to give a smooth batter. Season with one level teaspoon of sea salt and a quarter teaspoon of pepper.

4 Remove the foil, stir and cook for a further 10 minutes until the onion and sausage start to go brown. Add all the other ingredients to the roasting tin, mixing lightly. Place on your hob over a high heat until the contents start to sizzle, then pour in the batter.

5 Place in the oven and bake for about 40 minutes, until well-risen and golden.

I love to also make bubble and squeak with any veggies that didn't get eaten. See recipe on page 98.

This is such a brilliant way to use up some of the festive leftovers. I also serve this with the spiced beef on Boxing Day and make the mushroom and red wine jus to pour over everything.

Bubble and Squeak Cakes with Melting Cheese Pâté

Ingredients

600g mixed leftover cooked vegetables – needs to include 1/3 potato which can be mashed

1 medium free-range egg

1 teaspoon coarse grain or Dijon mustard

1 tablespoon chopped fresh herbs, such as chives, parsley or coriander

Sea salt and black pepper to taste

Coating

75g plain flour

2 medium eggs

Approximately 50ml water

200g breadcrumbs, panko are great

Sunflower oil for shallow frying

Cheese Pâté

150g cream cheese

50g of other cheeses such as cheddar, or a blue

1 tablespoon white wine

1 fat garlic clove, finely grated or puréed

A little chopped chilli

Fresh chopped herbs such as chives, coriander or parsley

Makes 12 cakes

What you do

1 Mash the left over potatoes and any other vegetable that may mash down, such as swede or celeriac. Finely chop the remaining veggies, such as carrot, cabbage, sprouts, parsnips etc. Tip into a bowl and mix together. Mix in the egg, mustard, herbs and seasoning.

2 Divide mixture into 12 portions and shape into small cakes.

Whisk the flour and eggs with enough water to form a batter into a single cream consistency. Dip into the breadcrumbs and pat the cakes to ensure they stick really well. Place in the fridge to firm up for about 20 minutes.

3 Meanwhile, make the cheese pâté by simply mixing all the ingredients together.

4 Heat a large frying pan with a good covering of sunflower oil.

5 Fry the bubble and squeak cakes in batches over a medium heat until a good golden colour on each side. Drain on kitchen paper and serve topped with a spoon of the cheese pâté.

The potted cheese pâté is a delicious addition to the bubble and squeak, however, if you are serving it to accompany other dishes then keep it simple with a good dollop of cranberry sauce, or try the watercress and horseradish sauce on page 95.

Posh Fish Pies

Ingredients

Base

1 pack filo pastry

Melted butter

Béchamel

750g milk

1 bay leaf

1 sprig thyme

1 stick celery, sliced

3 peppercorns

1 small carrot, sliced

60g butter

1 medium onion, finely chopped

1 tablespoon brandy

50ml white wine

60g plain flour

¼ teaspoon cayenne pepper

¼ teaspoon white pepper

1 teaspoon sea salt

1 flat teaspoon Dijon mustard

200ml crème fraîche

Fish filling

1 medium leek, shredded and sautéed

300g wilted spinach, well drained and buttered

400g white fish fillet

1 lobster tail, cooked

6 queenie scallops

50g smoked salmon, shredded

100g tight button mushrooms, sautéed

Topping

1.4kg whole floury potatoes, boiled in their skins until tender

90g butter

1 tablespoon crème fraîche

2 eggs

Salt, white pepper and nutmeg to season

6 king prawns

2 tablespoons of breadcrumbs and chopped herbs mixed together

Makes 6

What you do

1 First prepare the moulds. I use large American muffin tins, well buttered and lined with 3 layers of buttered filo, then part baked at 180°C/Fan 160°C/Gas 4 for about 15 minutes until lightly golden, but not too coloured.

2 Next make the béchamel sauce – Pour the milk into a pan, add the bay leaf, thyme, sliced celery, peppercorns and sliced carrot. Heat and bring to the boil, reduce to a gentle simmer for 5 minutes, then turn the heat off. Cover and leave to infuse until cooled.

3 Next, strain the milk into a jug or bowl. Melt the butter in a clean pan, add the onion and sauté until soft and straw coloured. Add the brandy and allow the alcohol to cook off, about 30 seconds, then add the wine and repeat. Stir in the flour, cayenne, white pepper, sea salt and mustard. Slowly whisk in the milk, continue stirring and bring to

the boil. Reduce to a simmer until thickened and stir in the crème fraîche.

4 Spoon some sautéed leek and wilted buttered spinach into the base of each filo pie shell. Half fill each with the sauce and then divide the fish, shellfish and mushrooms between the pies.

5 For the mash, peel the skins from the potatoes, push through a ricer into a bowl, season to taste, pour in the melted butter and crème fraîche, whip together and finish with grated nutmeg. Separate the eggs, whip in the yolks and whisk the whites until firm, then fold in. Spoon the mixture on top.

6 Finish with a whole prawn in each pie, inserting the tail end so the head is exposed and sprinkle with the breadcrumbs.

7 Bake at 200°C/Fan 180°C/Gas 6 until the potato is slightly puffed and golden, about 25 minutes.

Vegetarian Filling

Ingredients

50g butter

1 small onion, finely chopped

1 fat clove garlic, grated

50ml white wine

1 teaspoon Dijon mustard

Sea salt and black pepper

500g portobello mushrooms, cut into small chunks

6 chestnuts, chopped

A tablespoon of chopped parsley, sage or tarragon

120g blue cheese

What you do

1 Melt the butter and sauté the onion until soft. Stir in the garlic, wine and mustard and cook to reduce the wine by half. Season with ½ a teaspoon of sea salt and a ¼ teaspoon of black pepper, stir in the mushrooms and sauté until soft and a little coloured. Add the chestnuts, herbs and blue cheese and remove from the heat.

2 Now use this with the béchamel, sautéed leek and wilted buttered spinach as in the recipe on the previous page, finishing with the breadcrumbs and herbs.

Ginger Beer Gammon with a Pomegranate and Date Glaze

Christmas is not complete without a good piece of gammon to carve up over the festive holidays. This superbly sticky and flavourful recipe makes a great main course, but also the best sandwiches!

Ingredients

3.5kg gammon joint

2 litres good ginger ale or beer – enough to cover the meat

1 large sliced leek

1 medium onion, halved and studded with 4 cloves

1 large carrot, sliced

2 bay leaves

2 star anise

2 sticks celery, sliced

Glaze

12 cloves

4 tablespoons pomegranate molasses

4 tablespoons date molasses or molasses sugar

2 tablespoons maple syrup

To finish

2 tablespoons arrowroot

Serves 8-10

What you do

1 Check on the packaging whether the gammon needs pre-soaking.

2 Rinse the joint and place in a huge pan with all the ingredients. Bring to the boil and skim away any scum that forms with a slotted spoon. Reduce the heat to a gentle simmer and cook the gammon for approximately 3 hours (I use a meat thermometer; the internal temperature should be 70°C). Leave to cool in the liquid. Remove the gammon from the pan and place on a preparation board. Reserve the cooking stock. Use a sharp knife to take away the skin from the gammon.

3 Cut lines into the fat across the top and then go the other way to create mini diamonds. Stud with the cloves.

4 Mix together the pomegranate and date molasses with the maple syrup and spread all over the gammon.

5 Roast in the oven at 190°C/Fan 170°C/Gas 5, until a deep mahogany colour. Baste a couple of times throughout the cooking. This should take about 40 minutes.

6 Place the joint on a board to rest. Tip all the roasting juices into a saucepan, add enough reserved stock to take the measure to 500ml and bring to the boil. Dissolve the arrowroot in a little cooled leftover stock. Pour into the sauce, stirring all the time. It will thicken and become glossy. Check the seasoning, reduce the heat and keep warm whilst you carve the gammon.

Whenever I make this dish I have to make a potato gratin to go with it.

Simply boil 900g of potatoes until cooked through. Slice and place in a buttered ovenproof dish. Pour 1L of béchamel sauce over the top, finish with 75g of mature Cheddar and a sprinkle of breadcrumbs. Bake at 180°C/Fan 160°C/Gas 4 for 45 minutes until bubbling and golden, delish!

Christmas or New Year's Eve Seafood Extravaganza

Ingredients

Herb Butter

200g salted butter

1 teaspoon sea salt

½ teaspoon black pepper

1 teaspoon lemon zest, finely grated

2 large garlic cloves, finely grated

1 tablespoon parsley, chopped

1 tablespoon chives, chopped

24 large raw tiger prawns in their shells

8 king scallops in the half shell

400g piece of fish fillet e.g. monk, salmon, hake

2 cooked lobster, halved and dressed, claws cracked

To garnish

2 lemons, cut into 8 wedges

2 bunches watercress

Serves 8

What you do

1 Mix together the butter, sea salt, pepper, grated lemon zest, and garlic. Put the scallops on the half shells and dot a little of the butter mixture on each. Cover them with foil and place on a baking sheet. Cut the fish fillet into 8 portions, place on another tray lined with parchment and dot with a little of the butter mixture. Roast both the scallops and the fish in a preheated oven at 200°C/Fan 180°C/Gas 6 for 15 minutes. Remove, cover and rest for 5 minutes.

2 Meanwhile, cook the prawns. Heat the remaining butter in a large pan and when it begins to foam, but not brown, add the prawns and sauté until they turn deep pink. Remove from the heat, cover and keep warm.

3 Garnish a large platter with a bunch of watercress at each end and add the lemon wedges next to them. Remove the lobster tail meat from the tail shell, cut in half lengthways and pop back into the shell. Lay one at each end next to the watercress and lemons and place the claws next to the tails.

4 Place the scallops back on the half shells and arrange the prawns and fish fillets around them. Spoon any melted butter and juices from the cooking over the scallops, fish and prawns.

5 Serve with the aioli, the smoky tomato sauce and piles of thrice-fried chips. Now that's a feast!

Aioli

150ml good French style mayonnaise

100ml Greek yoghurt

4 cloves garlic, grated

1 teaspoon lemon zest

What you do

1 Simply mix the ingredients together, cover and chill until needed.

Smoky Tomato Sauce

400g tinned plum tomatoes

3 tablespoons olive oil

1 small onion, thinly sliced

1 flat teaspoon sea salt

½ teaspoon black pepper

1 mild red chilli, seeded and chopped finely

2 garlic cloves, grated

2 tablespoons fresh chopped coriander

1 tablespoon sweet smoked paprika

A pinch of dried chipotle chilli flakes

½ teaspoon of light soft brown sugar

What you do

❶ Chop the tinned tomatoes. Heat the oil in a large pan, add the onion and cook until softened and lightly golden. Season with the sea salt and black pepper.

❷ Add the tomatoes, plus the chilli, garlic, coriander, smoked paprika and chilli flakes. Simmer gently for about 40 minutes, until thickened. Sweeten a little with the sugar. Cool, cover and keep chilled until needed.

Once a Year Thrice Cooked Chips

Ingredients

10 large potatoes – use Maris Piper or Rooster

2 litres sunflower oil

100g goose fat

Serves 6-8

What you do

1 Peel the potatoes and cut into chips 5cm long by 1cm wide, place in a colander and rinse under cold water until the water runs clear.

2 Tip the chips into a large saucepan, cover with cold water and bring to a gentle simmer. Cook until soft to the touch but not cooked all the way through. Drain the chips and then cool under cold running water. Drain well and spread out onto a large tray. Chill in the fridge until dry and cold. This will take at least 30 minutes.

3 Heat the sunflower oil and goose fat together to 130°C; I use a deep saucepan and a thermometer.

4 Fry the chips in batches for 7–8 minutes, until a crust forms but without colour. Remove the chips and place on a baking tray. Chill in the fridge again for approximately 30 minutes. Once chilled, heat the oil and goose fat up to 180°C.

5 Deep-fry the chips in batches for a second time for 4–5 minutes, until crisp and golden – don't overcrowd the fryer as this will cause a drop in the oil temperature. Drain on absorbent kitchen towel and season with sea salt before serving.

Bûche de Noël

Ingredients

6 large eggs, separated

150g caster sugar

50g cocoa powder

60g self-raising flour

1 teaspoon vanilla extract

5 teaspoons icing sugar, to decorate

Filling

200g brandied sweet chestnut purée
– see recipe on page 121

50g unsalted butter

Ganache topping

500g good dark chocolate, finely chopped

450ml double cream

1 teaspoon vanilla bean paste

¼ teaspoon sea salt

Serves 8

What you do

1 Preheat the oven to 180°C/Fan 160°C/Gas 4.

In a large, clean bowl, whisk the egg whites until they form thick peaks, then, whilst still whisking, sprinkle in 50g of the caster sugar and continue whisking until the whites are holding their peaks but not dry.

2 In another bowl, whisk the egg yolks and the remaining caster sugar until the mixture is light, with a consistency like a pale, thick mousse. Add the vanilla extract, sieve the cocoa powder and self-raising flour and then gently but quickly fold in, reserving as much of the volume in the mixture as possible. Lighten the yolk mixture with a couple of dollops of the egg whites, folding them in thoroughly. Then add the remaining whites in thirds, folding them in carefully to avoid losing the air.

③ Line a Swiss roll tin with baking parchment, leaving a generous overhang at the ends and sides. Cut the parchment into the corners to help the paper fit and stay anchored.

④ Pour in the cake mixture and bake in the oven for 20 minutes, until firm to the touch. Remove from the oven and cool a little before turning it out onto another piece of baking parchment. If you dust this piece of parchment with a little icing sugar it may help prevent sticking, but don't worry too much as any tears or dents will be covered by the yummy chocolate covering later.

⑤ While the cake is baking, make the ganache. Heat the cream in a heavy-based pan until almost at boiling point. Remove from the heat and pour into the bowl with the chocolate. Add the vanilla and sea salt, leave for 2 minutes, then stir to combine.

⑥ For the filling, pour 200ml of the ganache into a bowl and add the unsalted butter. Stir in so it melts and combines. Uncover the cake and spread the surface with the brandied chestnut purée, followed by the ganache. Pick up the edges of the paper and lift up and over to make the first roll. Continue to roll forward now so you end up with the seal underneath. Cut away 1.5 inches from each end and use a little of the ganache topping to glue the pieces together, this will form a branch or stump. Place the log and branch on a wire rack with parchment underneath. Cover with a clean cloth, while the remaining ganache thickens up enough to spread and mould over the cake with control. You need to mix the ganache regularly with a spatula so it thickens evenly without lumps.

⑦ Once the ganache is easily spreadable, smooth thickly all over with a hot knife (use hot water to dip the knife in). Now use the knife to make bark markings all over for the log effect. Swirl the ends of the log and attach the branch, cover that and mark. Lightly dust with icing sugar and add some gold edible glitter for sparkle if you like. I like to add little chocolate mushrooms made with left over ganache – I dust them with cocoa powder and glitter, they eat like truffles!

8 Cover and keep in the fridge for up to 48 hours, or freeze for up to 6 weeks.

This is a French classic that I learned to master when I worked in Paris. It has become a real favourite with my family of chocoholics!

Sweet Chestnut Purée

Ingredients

75ml of water

175g of caster sugar

1 teaspoon of vanilla bean paste

1 tablespoon of brandy

300g of cooked chestnuts

What you do

1 Make a syrup by boiling 75ml of water with the caster sugar for 10 minutes.

2 Remove from the heat and cool slightly. Stir in the vanilla bean paste and brandy.

2 Using a food processor, blitz the cooked chestnuts, add the syrup and continue to blend until a smooth purée is formed.

Almond and
Fruit Jalousie

Ingredients

Frangipane

85g unsalted butter at room temperature – it should be nice and soft

85g golden caster sugar

85g ground almonds

50g plain flour

1 medium egg

1 teaspoon vanilla paste

Jalousie

1 pack ready-made puff pastry

220g mincemeat

1 large eating apple, peeled, thinly sliced and sautéed in 20g of butter to soften

1 tablespoon brandy or rum

1 medium size egg, beaten for glazing

1 dessertspoon of demerara sugar

To Serve

Icing sugar to dust

Crème fraîche to serve

Serves 8

What you do

1 First make the frangipane by mixing everything together into a thick paste.

2 Roll the pastry to a thin oblong, 6 inches wide and 18 inches long. Cut in half crosswise to give you 2 x 9 inch long strips. Flour one strip lightly and fold in half lengthways. Make a series of evenly spaced cuts through the folded edges to within one inch of the trimmed edge on both sides. This will give a glimpse of the mincemeat and apples inside, once placed on top and baked.

3 To assemble the jalousie, line a large baking sheet with parchment paper. Place the base pastry on the baking sheet and spread with the frangipane, leaving an inch border all the way around. Spoon the mincemeat on top and smooth out to cover the frangipane. Next, lay a line of overlapping cooked apple slices along the centre of the mincemeat and spoon over the rum.

Brush the edge of the base all around with some egg wash. Open out the slashed piece of pastry and lay on top. Seal the edges all around and crimp them together. Brush with some egg wash and sprinkle with the demerara sugar.

4 Place in the centre of a preheated oven at 190°C/Fan 170°C/Gas 5 and bake for 25 to 30 minutes, until well risen and beautifully golden. If you think it is browning too quickly you may reduce the oven temperature for the last 5 to 10 minutes and cover with a sheet of foil. Remove from the oven. Dredge lightly with icing sugar and serve warm with some crème fraîche.

Baked Nutcracker Cheesecake

Cheesecake has become one of the nation's favourite desserts. This one pulls out all the stops with a seasonal twist of nut brittle and salted caramel.

Ingredients

Base

175g of biscuits – try ginger snaps, hobnobs or amaretti

50g unsalted melted butter

25g caster sugar

Cheesecake

600g full fat Philadelphia cream cheese

120g golden caster sugar

1 teaspoon vanilla bean paste

1 teaspoon orange zest

4 medium free-range eggs, beaten

60ml soured cream

Nutcracker

150g pecan nuts or whole almonds

100g caster sugar

Caramel

65g unsalted butter

160g caster sugar

100ml double cream

1 teaspoon vanilla bean paste

¼ teaspoon sea salt

To finish

1 dessertspoon icing sugar

½ teaspoon ground cinnamon

Serves 8

· ·

What you do

1 Preheat the oven to 140°C/Fan 120°C/Gas 1 and line a 20cm spring form cake tin.

2 To make the base, break the biscuits into a food processor and whizz to form fine crumbs, drizzle in the melted butter and stir in the sugar. Spoon into the base of the lined tin and pat down evenly.

3 To make the cheesecake filling – place the cream cheese, sugar, vanilla and orange zest in a mixing bowl and briefly mix together using an electric whisk. Add the eggs one at a time, whisking between each, and then the soured cream. Pour into the cake tin and bake for 60-70 minutes, until set. Remove and leave to cool at room temperature, then place in the fridge to chill for 2 hours. Decant the cheesecake onto a serving stand or dish.

4 Now make the nutcracker – Place the pecans or almonds on a baking sheet and roast in the oven at 140°C/Fan 120°C/Gas 1 for 15 minutes, remove and set aside. Line a baking sheet with parchment. Pour the sugar into a heavy-based pan and cook to form a light golden caramel, stir in the pecans or almonds, then pour onto the lined baking sheet. Leave to set, then break up roughly with a large chopping knife.

5 To make the caramel sauce, put the butter and sugar in a heavy-based pan. Keep stirring until the mixture turns a golden caramel colour, then slowly whisk in the cream, vanilla and sea salt. Let it

bubble and thicken before removing it from the heat and leave to cool.

6 To complete the look of the cheesecake, mix together the icing sugar/cinnamon and dust the edges and sides with it, then spoon over the caramel sauce, followed by the nutcracker.

7 This will keep in the fridge for up to 3 days – the cheesecake can be frozen for up to 6 weeks. I would do this without the topping.

The caramel sauce is delicious and I sometimes make a couple of jars and keep them in the fridge for ice cream, pancakes or even Greek yoghurt topped with some toasted nuts.

Ginger Pudding with Chocolate Orange Sauce and Praline Crumb

This dessert is my over the top homage to a certain round chocolate orange, which I first tasted in my grandparents shop in the early 70s. I have served it several times as an alternative to Christmas pudding, accompanied by a small glass of Tawny Port or Penderyn whisky.

Ingredients

Sponge

175g unsalted butter, softened

175g light muscovado sugar

1 tablespoon syrup from a jar of stem ginger

3 large free-range eggs, beaten

175g self-raising flour

1 teaspoon baking powder

1 teaspoon ground ginger

Sauce

100g dark chocolate

100ml double cream

1½ teaspoon ground cinnamon

1 tablespoon orange juice

1 tablespoon orange zest

Praline

125g caster sugar

50g flaked almonds

1 teaspoon lemon juice

Serves 6

....

What you do

1 To make the sponges – Cream the butter and sugar until light and fluffy. Add the syrup, then the eggs, then fold in the flour, baking powder and ginger.

2 Divide between 6 buttered pudding moulds, tightly covering each with foil. Place in a roasting tin and pour in enough water to reach halfway up the sides of the moulds. Cover the tin with foil and bake in the oven at 180°C/Fan 160°C/Gas 4 for 25 minutes.

3 For the praline – Melt the caster sugar in a frying pan until it turns golden or reaches 300°C/570°F on a sugar thermometer – take care here as the sugar will be very hot. Add the almonds and lemon juice, stir well and then spoon onto a silicon-lined baking sheet. Leave to cool and then cut into wedges with a sharp knife. Place in a food processor and briefly blitz to form a crumb finish.

4 To make the sauce – Break the chocolate into a heatproof bowl over a saucepan of simmering water (to act as a double boiler) and slowly melt it with the double cream, cinnamon and orange juice and zest. Once it is melted, remove from the heat and stir to create a thick but runny chocolate sauce. If it is too thick, try adding a drop of hot water and stir in well.

5 To serve, run a knife around the inside of the moulds and decant onto dessert plates. Spoon the chocolate orange sauce over the top and sprinkle a good helping of praline to finish.

6 Serve with whipped double cream, crème fraîche or my favourite of a scoop of vanilla ice cream.

To make a larger version of this pudding, I use a buttered 600ml basin and steam it on a trivet in a large covered saucepan for about 1 hour. Check it is cooked through by inserting a skewer into the centre. If it comes out with sponge mixture on it, you will need to cook it a little longer, perhaps 10-15 minutes.

Midnight
Pears

Ingredients

6 pears, preferably Comice or Williams

Filling

100g Medjool dates, chopped finely

100g dried soft figs, chopped finely

50g soft dried apricots, chopped finely

2 tablespoons of crème de cassis

Poaching Liquid

1 bottle of nice Merlot or Cabernet

Water

1 bay leaf

2 strips of orange peel

2 star anise

2 cloves

2 cracked cardamom pods

150g dark brown sugar

200ml crème de cassis

Serves 6

What you do

1 Using a small sharp knife, mark a collar in the skin around the top of each pear, then peel away the skin from the collar to the base. Take a slim slice off the base of the pear so that it stands up and use a "melon-baller", or the point of a small knife to scoop out the core and the pips, working from the bottom up.

2 Mix together the filling and stuff the pears. Stand them upright in a saucepan just large enough to hold them snugly. Pour in the wine and enough water to cover them – the storks can be visible. Add the bay leaf, orange peel, star anise, cloves, cardamoms, and sugar. Slowly bring to the boil, then cover and simmer until the pears are soft through, about 20-30 minutes.

3 Remove the pears with a slotted spoon and sit them in a bowl.

4 Turn up the heat under the liquid and reduce by half. Pour in the crème de cassis and pour over the pears. Leave to cool, cover and refrigerate for 48 hours so they turn blackish purple.

5 Remove from the fridge 20 minutes before serving.

6 I like to serve them with chai cookies (recipe on page 140) and crème fraîche.

I usually make these 4 days in advance of serving them so that they really take on the colour and flavour of the wine, spices and cassis.

Chai Cookies and Chai Spice Mix

I love this spice mix! It is superbly aromatic and warming. I use it in so many dishes, from shortbread to sweetened butter, which I serve with mince pies. A teaspoonful will also make a stunning latte!

Chai Cookies

Ingredients

300g unsalted butter, cut into small pieces, softened

150g caster sugar, plus extra for dredging

300g plain flour

150g rice flour

2 tablespoons chai spice mix (see next page)

To finish

1 x 397g tin ready made caramel

2 tablespoons icing sugar

1 teaspoon chai spice mix

Makes 36

....

What you do

1 To make melt-in-the-mouth shortbread, you need a really good-quality unsalted butter, so don't skimp on this and never use margarine. For that delectable, friable texture, it is also important to keep a light hand – overworking the mixture will make the dough oily and the shortbread tough. And finally, shortbread must be only barely coloured, so don't forget it's in the oven!

2 Preheat the oven to 170°C/Fan 150°C/Gas 3.

3 Put the softened butter into a bowl. Using a wooden spoon, gradually work in the sugar until it is well mixed and forms a soft paste. Sift in the flours and spice and, using a fork, bring together lightly to form a soft, crumbly dough. Then bring the mix to a soft, pliable, crack-free dough by kneading it as lightly as possible. Wrap and chill for an hour.

4 For the biscuits, place the dough between two sheets of lightly floured greaseproof paper. Using a rolling pin, roll out to a 5mm thickness. Remove the top paper and cut out biscuits using a 6–7cm fluted cutter or a shaped biscuit cutter. Place the biscuits on the baking sheets and prick the surface of each with a fork.

5 Bake the shortbread in the oven until very lightly coloured; allow about 20 minutes for the biscuits. Cool on a rack, then spoon half the biscuits with a little of the caramel and sandwich with another, dust with the icing sugar and spice mixed together and eat!

Chai Spice Mix

Ingredients

½ tablespoon black peppercorns

2 tablespoons whole cinnamon sticks, broken up into small pieces

1 tablespoon cardamom pods

1 tablespoon whole cloves

1 whole nutmeg, broken up with a rolling pin; I pop it under a tea-towel

2 tablespoons ground ginger

Makes approximately 100g

What you do

1 Heat a small pan over a medium to high heat. Add the peppercorns, cinnamon pieces, cardamom pods, cloves and nutmeg pieces.

2 Roast briefly until aromatic, stir the spices and shake the pan so they roast evenly.

3 Tip into a bowl to cool and then blitz to a powder in a spice grinder, or have a good work out using a mortar and pestle!

4 Tip the spice powder back into the bowl, stir in the ground ginger and then keep in a small screw or clip top jar.

5 Use to make a delicious latte, season poached fruits or mix with icing sugar and sift over stollen and mince pies.

Christmas
Pudding

Ingredients

100g mixed dried fruits e.g. raisins, sultanas

50g dried cranberries

30g chopped candied orange peel

The zest of 2 clementines, plus 4 tablespoons of juice

1 zest of a lemon, plus 2 tablespoons of juice

2 tablespoons brandy or cognac

100g unsalted butter, softened, plus a little for buttering the pudding basin

100g dark muscovado sugar

50g self-raising flour

1 tablespoon cocoa powder

1 teaspoon mixed spice

½ teaspoon ground ginger

2 medium eggs

1 medium eating apple, peeled, cored and grated

2 nuggets of stem ginger, chopped

50g white breadcrumbs

50g dark glacé cherries, chopped (optional)

85g good quality dark chocolate, chopped

Serves 8-10

What you do

1 Put the dried mixed fruit, cranberries, zests of the clementine and lemon, plus the juices and brandy in a bowl, mix well, cover and soak in the fridge for 3 days, stirring daily.

2 To make the pudding – Butter a 1 litre pudding basin and line the bottom with a disc of greaseproof paper.

3 In a mixing bowl, beat together the butter and sugar until pale and fluffy. Sift in the flour, cocoa and spice, ground ginger and combine. Fold in the eggs one at a time, followed by the grated apple, stem ginger, the soaked fruits, breadcrumbs, cherries and chocolate. Mix thoroughly.

4 Fill the basin with the mixture and cover with a double thickness of greaseproof paper, pleated in the middle. Cover this with a layer of foil, again pleated in the middle, then secure tightly around the top of the basin with string.

5 Place the pudding in a large saucepan on a trivet or upturned saucer so it doesn't touch the bottom. Fill the pan with enough hot water to reach halfway up the basin. Place over a medium/high heat and bring to a simmer, cover the pan and gently simmer for 2 hours.

6 If you are preparing your pudding in advance, cool completely once cooked and keep in a cool, dark place or in the fridge (I make two and keep one for the following year).

7 To reheat, steam for 1 hour, or remove foil, decant onto a plate, cover with cling film, pierce in several places and microwave on full power for 4 minutes. Leave to stand for 2 minutes before serving.

I love the tradition of adding a little trinket to the pudding. In 2016 The Royal Mint produced a beautiful little sixpence, which I used in my pudding. It's worth checking their website to see what they have on offer this year.

The festive season at the school

The festive season at the Cookery School is a very busy time for our team. We start our count down at the beginning of November and from there on, it's a fast track to the end of the year. Organisation is paramount in delivering our events and classes.

We host a number of demonstration events designed to immerse our guests in festive cheer. It is such a pleasure to entertain them and share tales of Christmas adventures past. Food is the key to everything here, the dishes I choose to demonstrate assist me to tell my stories and I love to have fun with it all. I have already mentioned the word "organisation", and in the lead up to one of these events, there is much to do.

It all starts 2 days before; these are our longest days of the year in the kitchen, starting at 5am with tea and hot bacon and mushroom rolls. There is always a lovely calm atmosphere as we begin to gather what we need for the great make and bake day.

We have pre-orders from our customers to take care of and a general mix of festive goodies for people to buy on the day. We usually start with our once a year raised pork pies, then move on to the doughs that will make the cinnamon and cardamom butter kringle wreaths, fruit, cheese and nut wreaths and the porcini and truffle bread. Then the sweet selection; jalousies, ginger cake with candied orange, chai and caramel cookie

bags and chocolate Christmas cake with bronze popping candy and pistachios.

A few weeks before this, we would have made our pickles, chutneys, cranberry sauces, pickled pears and our own mincemeat. Everything gets beautifully wrapped in cellophane and finished off with pretty ribbon and hand-written labels. When it's all laid out, it looks fabulous!

On the second preparation day, we don't leave until we are happy that the scene is set to welcome our guests in the morning. Tables are laid, glasses are lined up on trays ready for bubbly, canapés are on trays in the fridge, ready to cook off first thing, and the mulled wine infuses overnight with aromatic spices and citrus.

Then comes the morning and the air is filled with the aroma of mulled wine and coffee. The demonstration area is set with festive props and trays of ingredients for each recipe, all prepared and ready to be magically transformed into a delicious feast. We all take a moment to have a coffee and a quick nibble as we check through the running order, just one more time.

Cue the festive music as we open the doors to our guests. They jostle their way in so they can get a good look at the spread of edible gifts. Everything feverishly disappears into white paper carrier bags that are labelled and stored for later collection. It really is a wonderful sight, and we love the fact that our once a year specials are shared with so many people, it is a great feeling.

Our team gets busy serving sweet and savoury treats with mulled wine or coffee as guests arrive at their tables. Everyone relaxes themselves into their seats and before we know it, it's SHOWTIME! People are genuinely excited to see how my culinary acrobatics and wizardry will all turn out.

Three-quarters of the way through my demonstration marathon we break to serve bubbly and canapés. The finale features a parade of eye-popping desserts and I can feel the room adding up the calories and saving up their dietary sins so they can indulge!

Next comes our festive lunch. We replicate two dishes that have been demonstrated for a main course and dessert. Following this, great excitement builds in the room as we head for the highlight of the day.

All in all, I usually demonstrate around 10 showstopper dishes, which then go into our infamous charity raffle. It really is quite a spectacle, with people whooping and cheering for the winners, who march off with enormous eats such as whole salmon and spiced pilaf en croute, or a spectacular triple-decker nutcracker cheesecake wrapped in spun sugar.

At the end of it all, we are exhausted, but elated. It's testimony to just how good my team are, how we all love food, entertaining and working together.

We also run a series of Christmas themed hands-on classes, where people can come along and make some impressive dishes of their own which they take home and freeze ahead of the big day.

These have become so popular over the years, with people booking as early as January to ensure their place in November and December. I think the reason behind this is that they can totally immerse themselves in the experience and, with our expert guidance, make things that they perhaps wouldn't try at home.

When we reach the end of our School year, we have our own Christmas and New Year celebrations to look forward to and each of us will be doing something different. It's a time to recharge the batteries, take stock and get some head space before we open the School once more in January. The first 4 months of the year are very busy, as Father Christmas is so thoughtful in treating lots of people to a cookery course with us. Thank you, Santa!

Be stress-free!

The best advice I can give you is to be realistic in what you can handle and to set aside enough time to prepare and enjoy the whole process.

Be organised

Plan your menus, think how many times you will be entertaining and for how many people. Next, choose your menus for each occasion; keep it simple with one or two showstopper mains and a few delicious side dishes. If it's drinks and nibbles, you can do all of the food way in advance.

Make lists

Next, make your shopping lists, using headings so they are detailed. You can buy your store cupboard and frozen ingredients well ahead of time. It will be a good idea to order some fresh ingredients in advance, especially something special like goose, turkey or seafood. Other fresh ingredients can then be brought or ordered nearer the time. In addition to the ingredients, think of other things you might need, such as foil

of time e.g. make your Christmas pudding, cake, mince pies, canapés and even your "pigs in blankets" as early as October. Why not make some pickles and chutneys too if you have time, they make great gifts.

Plan the execution

Don't get overwhelmed! I always begin my preparations with a pre-Christmas organisation of my kitchen. I check cupboards, drawers and surfaces, freeing up as much space as possible and keeping the equipment I will need to hand.

Look at your entertaining schedule; even if it is just Christmas Day, it needs to be planned. Organise what you can do in advance. You will need to work out the timings for your turkey/goose/beef etc. so that you know when you need to start on the actual day. Once that is underway, your timings for everything else should be less stressful, especially if you get a lot done in advance. Here's a basic guideline.

containers for freezing canapés, extra baking parchment, freezer bags, clip or screw top jars and foil. Then the pretty things like napkins, candles, flowers etc. It is so satisfying to tick these things off your list.

Make ahead

As I explained in my introduction, there is so much you can do ahead

2 days before

Defrost anything for Christmas Day safely in the fridge. A large turkey or ballotine of goose may take longer, so take it out 3 days in advance. Make things like spiced red cabbage, cranberry sauce, bread sauce, stuffing, stock for gravy.

Day before

Time to gather helping hands (even if reluctant) to the table and prepare the vegetables. This is a ritual in our house and mulled wine and nibbles keep us all going, even if it's in the morning! You can then par-boil the potatoes, blanch sprouts, carrots, parsnips, cool and cover to store in the fridge. If you are making Yorkshire pudding or Festive Toad, you can make the batter the day before and keep it in the fridge. I do all of this in the morning, as I want my kitchen clear and ready for Christmas Eve supper.

On the day

Follow your timetable, putting the meat in to cook first. Roast potatoes, parsnips, stuffing and pigs in blankets can go in towards the end of cooking, or even whilst the meat is resting. You will have at least 40 minutes available to do these jobs before carving. Loosely cover the meat with foil and pile a few tea towels on top to keep the meat cosy. Finish the fresh vegetables, those you have blanched the day before can be finished in boiling water. It's time to make the gravy too: use the meat juices (spoon off most of the fat) and the stock you have prepared or brought. Make sure you have warm serving dishes and plates. If you don't have room in the oven, put everything in the dishwasher without a tablet and pop it on a short cycle. Do this when you take the meat out, that way the dishes will all be hot and ready to use.

Finally, don't forget to leave time to get yourself ready! I usually escape for 20 minutes and relax with a glass of bubbly before taking to the kitchen for the grand finale. Have fun!

About Angela Gray

Angela opened the Cookery School at Llanerch Vineyard in 2011. The School also hosts a number of special events where Angela cooks, chats enthusiastically and promotes the good life through cooking and eating together.

Everything that precedes her time at the School has given her the wealth of experience and knowledge needed to head such an ambitious project. She worked prolifically in the food world, starting her career as a personal chef working in Europe and North America. Her clients included an esteemed list, from European aristocracy to high profile clients such as Lord Lloyd Webber. Angela took to the helm at a number of restaurants, where she developed her relaxed style of cuisine with a strong Mediterranean influence.

She returned home to Wales, where her career path changed when she attended university in Cardiff and gained a BSc Honours degree in food science. Whilst studying, Angela also ran a small catering business and held a twice-monthly Cooking Club from her home. This would later form the basis of two prime time cookery series for BBC Wales, *Hot Stuff* and *More Hot Stuff*. Next came several series for radio, including *My Life on a Plate* and *Packed Lunch*. She still loves to get involved in media projects, but her main focus these days is at the School and writing her cookery books.

At the close of 2016 the School was listed in the top 10 Cookery Schools in *The Independent*, *The Telegraph*, *Sunday Times* and *Evening Standard*. Most recently it was also chosen for the prestigious *National Cookery School Guide*. In her own words, that's the result of team work at its best.

Dedication

Once again for my mum Betty, who made all our Christmases so very special, and for my lovely family, thank heavens we all love food. See you at Christmas!

Thanks

A huge thank you to Huw for the beautiful pictures once again and giving those cheeky little mice of mine a star turn. Huw can vouch that the gin cured salmon is delicious; he took it home and ate the lot, with the help of some friends.

A huge thanks again to Pamela, who crossed all my T's and dotted all my I's whilst in Portugal. She did it all seated in an inflatable chair, floating on a lovely pool in the sunshine, ably assisted by lots of chilled wine!

To my apprentice Ross, who has such a creative flair and was a great assistant on the photo shoot.

Thanks to Sarah for organising the additional photos and to all the team at Graffeg, especially Peter and Joana.

Finally, thank you to all my team at the School: Pam, Sarah, Carole, Susan, Sian, JoAnne and Ross. I am blessed!

Angela's Recommendations

- Cariad Wine at Llanerch Vineyard.
- Wally's Delicatessen, Cardiff.
- Ashton Fishmongers, Cardiff.
- Paleo Nutrition, Llandeilo.
- Martin Player, Cardiff.
- Halen Môn Sea Salt.
- Dyfi Distillery, Corris, Mid Wales.
- Welsh Whisky Company.

Metric and imperial equivalents

Weights	Solid
15g	$\frac{1}{2}$oz
25g	1oz
40g	$1\frac{1}{2}$oz
50g	$1\frac{3}{4}$oz
75g	$2\frac{3}{4}$oz
100g	$3\frac{1}{2}$oz
125g	$4\frac{1}{2}$oz
150g	$5\frac{1}{2}$oz
175g	6oz
200g	7oz
250g	9oz
300g	$10\frac{1}{2}$oz
400g	14oz
500g	1lb 2oz
1kg	2lb 4oz
1.5kg	3lb 5oz
2kg	4lb 8oz
3kg	6lb 8oz

Volume	Liquid
15ml	$\frac{1}{2}$ floz
30ml	1 floz
50ml	2 floz
100ml	$3\frac{1}{2}$ floz
125ml	4 floz
150ml	5 floz ($\frac{1}{4}$ pint)
200ml	7 floz
250ml	9 floz
300ml	10 floz ($\frac{1}{2}$ pint)
400ml	14 floz
450ml	16 floz
500ml	18 floz
600ml	1 pint (20 floz)
1 litre	$1\frac{3}{4}$ pints
1.2 litre	2 pints
1.5 litre	$2\frac{3}{4}$ pints
2 litres	$3\frac{1}{2}$ pints
3 litres	$5\frac{1}{4}$ pints

Angela's Cookbooks

Angela's cookbooks bring together a collection of recipes inspired by the seasons, her childhood, travels and career in food. They also form the basis of many of the courses run at her Cookery School at Llanerch Vineyard in the Vale of Glamorgan.

Winter Recipes

Everything naturally warms up in colour and flavour in this recipe collection. Angela uses a wide range of ingredients to invigorate the palette, from aromatic spice blends to the punchy flavours of pomegranate molasses, porcini and truffle.

Spring Recipes

Expect fresh, zesty flavours, vibrant colours and lots of inspiring ways to enhance your day-to-day cooking at home.

Summer Recipes

This book features a rich collection of recipes from Angela's travels and her time spent working in the South of France. Barbecuing, dining al fresco, entertaining friends, it's all here.

Autumn Recipes

Colours and flavours become richer and deeper in this book and recipes embrace the wonderful harvest of seasonal ingredients. Angela shares easy ways to entertain so you can be the host with the most.

Festive Recipes

The highlight of the Cookery School calendar is the 'Festive Kitchen' event, where Angela demonstrates a range of inspirational recipes that are all showstoppers, guaranteed to 'wow' friends and family throughout the Christmas and New Year celebrations. This is her very special collection of those recipes.

'Success on a plate is all in the planning. Keep things simple, make as much ahead of time as possible, and enjoy!'